IT FEELS
GOOD
TO BE PUNCTUAL
AT HOME

This book is dedicated
to all of you punctual kids
at home so that your Mom & Dad
can really be proud of you.
Thank you!

I am Mandy.

I am punctual when I
use my wrist watch.

I am Peter.

I am punctual when I set my alarm clock and wake up in the morning without trouble.

I am Chloe.

I am punctual when I
shut down my light and go
to sleep at a reasonable time
in the evening.

I am Karim.

I am punctual when I help out
my little brother with learning about
reading the time the right way.

I am Lola.

I am punctual when I don't deceive my parents and keep the light shut down without hiding under the sheets and reading my favorite book.

I am Edward.

I am punctual when I listen closely when my Mom and Dad tell me the time when I have to be at home.

I am Jennifer.

I am punctual when I write down my schedule of chores at home.

I am Patrick.

I am punctual when I cheer up my little sister and help her get dressed quickly so that both of us are not late.

I am Brenda.

I am punctual when I treat my wrist watch in a thoughtful manner so that it does not get broken because with a broken wrist watch I can not be punctual.

I am Claudia.

I am punctual when I share
the time with my friends so neither
of us gets home late.

I feel happy and good
about myself when
I am punctual and
when I respect
the time!

CPSIA information can be obtained
at www.ICGtesting.com
Printed in the USA
BVHW061058270519
549345BV00026B/2532